DELAYS ALL LEADERS MUST CONTEND WITH

*Understanding God's
Timing and Faithfulness*

LIFE IMPACT SERIES

FRANK DAMAZIO

CityChristianPublishing

www.CityChristianPublishing.com

PUBLISHED BY CITY CHRISTIAN PUBLISHING
9200 NE Fremont, Portland, Oregon 97220

City Christian Publishing is a ministry of City Bible Church and is dedicated to serving the local church and its leaders through the production and distribution of quality equipping resources. It is our prayer that these materials, proven in the context of the local church, will equip leaders in exalting the Lord and extending His kingdom.

For a free catalog of additional resources from City Christian Publishing, please call 1-800-777-6057 or visit our web site at www.citychristianpublishing.com.

Delays All Leaders Must Contend With
© Copyright 2006 by Frank Damazio
All Rights Reserved
ISBN 13: 978-1-59383-046-5
ISBN 10: 1-59383-046-7

Cover design by DesignPoint, Inc.

First Edition, January 2006

Printed in the United States of America

CONTENTS

When our well-laid plans seem to stall without reason, we must in faith submit our expectations and timing to the will of God. Perhaps most challenging, we must suppress the desire to take matters into our own hands.

Contradictions in life and ministry are numerous and are part of God's sovereign school for shaping great leaders through periods of delayed fulfillment.

A negative attitude contributes greatly to delays in blessings. The heart of a fruitful ministry is a heart of unconditional love for God and for all people.

Jealousy and envy are rooted in our worldly need to compare ourselves and our ministries to others. These emotions are among the most subtle and potent weapons in satan's arsenal and may become an obstacle to our spiritual progress.

Chapter 1

DELAYS THAT TEST FAITH

The airport was packed and I was late for my connecting flight. I was anxious to get off the plane and race to my connecting gate. The flight attendant had asked for those not connecting to let the other passengers go first, but no one seemed to be moved by her request for mercy. Everyone packed the aisles and it was slow moving. I wouldn't normally have been that concerned, but my connection was an overseas flight, and if I missed it, my whole itinerary would change.

Finally off, I raced with my carry-on bag and briefcase down the airport runway and over to the international wing. I was sweating, out of breath, and very anxious. At the counter I asked, "Excuse me. Excuse me. Has flight 119 already departed?" A smiling United worker pointed over to the reader board. The words were easy to see: DELAYED! Feeling a little embarrassed, I slipped away from the counter for a good laugh. All that worry, work, and unplanned exercise, and the flight had been delayed.

Delays Can Be a Blessing

This was one of those few times that being delayed was a blessing. Usually I hate the thought of being interrupted, slowed down, or stopped. The other word I cringe at is "canceled"—when traveling, that is. The reason is that canceled usually just means more waiting. No one really enjoys waiting: waiting in lines, waiting at doctors' offices, waiting for answers from people we've written. Even being left on hold bothers some people.

You and I know well that life has many surprising delays, most without warning. To be delayed 15 minutes is tolerable; after an hour, we're ready to cry "unjust"; a day or more of waiting is a nightmare worthy of repeating to your grandchildren later in life! What would you do with 39 years of delays? Thirty-nine years of waiting?

That's how long Sarah and Abraham waited for God to deliver his promise to them. Abraham was already in his seventies when God again told him that his children, his family and their seed, would eventually populate the world, numerous as "the dust of the earth." But Sarah remained childless through the passing years, and she and Abraham would grow much older as they waited for God to change their situation.

At last, as recorded in Genesis 21:1-2, "the Lord visited Sarah as He had said, and the Lord did for Sarah as He had spoken. For Sarah conceived and bore Abraham a son in his old age, at the set time of which God had spoken." Abraham was 100 when his son Isaac was born, and Sarah was 90 as she nursed her promised child.

Even in biblical times, the birth of a child to a 100-year-old man and his 90-year-old wife was considered impossible. Sarah, in fact, laughed about it. "All who hear about this will laugh with me. For who would have dreamed that I would ever have a baby?" (Gen. 21:6-7). But while it was in human terms "impossible," the supernatural power of God made the birth possible. Where there was no hope, no possibility, no natural resources, God gave a miracle.

Refining Faith in the Furnace of Life

The life of Abraham and Sarah was a lesson in the school of delayed promises. The lessons they learned were not mastered in a classroom, but in the furnace of life. Abraham and Sarah's faith struggles are recorded in Scripture to encourage all who believe and remain faithful during seasons of delay, silence, and unfruitfulness. The life of faith is built around promises given, tests encountered, and fulfillment enjoyed. For every promise, there is a test, and with every test there is grace, mercy, and the strength of the Almighty to see us through (Ps. 105:19).

Sarah and Abraham received clear promises, indicating what God would do for them in their unproductive condition. Both responded, but their responses lacked the one and only element that could deliver them from their season of delay—faith.

Their first response was in the realm of reasoning rather than faith. To reason correctly is to infer from propositions that are known or evident to a natural conclusion. However, people may reason wrongly as well as rightly. Abraham and Sarah had to go through—as do all who receive a vision, word, or promise from God—the reasoning test.

The Reasoning Test

As with most tests, the reasoning test has multiple-choice solutions that are often masked in partial truths and then complicated by human error. Let's look at some of them.

Religious Reasoning

Genesis 16:2 says, "Now behold, the Lord has prevented me from bearing children" (*NASB*). Sarah's reasoning was partially right and partially wrong. The Lord had not prevented her from having children *forever*. The delay was not a conclusion to the matter. It was a case of divine timing. Religious reasoning caused Sarah to take the matter into her own hands and to devise a plan for fulfilling God's promise. Sarah reasoned and rejected the faith-miracle factor that God could, at His choosing, give her a child. She instead concocted a plan, using her handmaid to produce a child named Ishmael, to fulfill God's promise. The problem: God will not honor our remedies.

Good Source Reasoning

Genesis 16:2 tells us, "And Abraham listened to the voice of Sarai" (*NASB*). Sarah had an influential voice in this matter. She was the suffering woman, the beloved wife of Abraham. Surely God would honor what this frustrated and humble woman of God desired. Her plan had earmarks of something God could use to put a stop to all of this delay business. Besides, God had been silent concerning the issue, so it was now Sarah and Abraham's responsibility to carry on the vision, they believed. This wrong reasoning would hinder the plans and purposes of God, and birth Ishmael, whose offspring would be a thorn in Israel's side for generations to come. God had not been the initiator of Sarah's idea and would not use Ishmael to fulfill His promise.

Natural Instinct Reasoning

Genesis 16:1-3 shows that after 10 years in Canaan, Sarah was still sterile. The promise was still unfulfilled. Sarah in her "natural instinct" reasoning simply suggested that they take matters into their own hands. The carnal mind always seeks to aid God's working. Unbelief is prolific with creative schemes. There was no human hope that the promise could be accomplished in the form in which they had first understood it. And yet it is always hard to resist the temptation to bow to natural reasoning, especially when it appeals to natural instincts.

Cultural Reasoning

Genesis 16:1 states, "And she had an Egyptian maidservant whose name was Hagar." Sarah had within her household an answer to her problem, and what Sarah proposed was a very common practice in those days. Ancient tablets containing marriage contracts discovered by archaeologists specify that a barren woman was required to provide a woman for her husband for the purpose of procreation. This idea was not sinful in and of itself. It was an acceptable cultural practice to handle what seemingly could not be changed—sterility. Abraham had allowed thought patterns and practices that he had learned from his pagan culture to influence his thinking. But God wanted Abraham and Sarah to use faith, the "God answer" in their circumstance, not Hagar, the "cultural answer."

The Challenge Never Changes: Trust and Obey

The modern-day unfulfilled church or ministry experiences all of the same problems Sarah and Abraham had to face, embrace, and surrender to God for a remedy. Leaders will encounter the reasoning test during delays of vision fulfillment and a "God silence."

What is challenged? Our ability to trust God's Word, God's ways, and God's simplicity, which is at times mind-boggling, in methods of building His Church. Religious reasoning, good source reasoning, natural instinct reasoning, and cultural reasoning may be some of the greatest obstacles we leaders will face before seeing God move mightily in our ministries and churches.

At times it is easier to follow our natural inclination and cultural wisdom and to use our own resources to bring the blessing we so desperately desire. We may yield to methodology, managerial paradigms, and leading-edge concepts for our numerical growth. These are not sinful in and of themselves, but without faith (the spiritual element that God responds to), all of these things are Ishmaels. Romans 14:23 tells us that "whatever is not from faith is sin." Buildings, programs, ideas, creative evangelism, seeker-sensitive innovation may all fall into the Ishmael category.

Joseph Stowell states this fact quite eloquently in his book *Shepherding the Church into the Twenty-First Century:*

Unfortunately, hitting the mark these days is tougher than it has ever been. The dramatic shift of our society has tended to blur vision and divide our focus. The shift is disoriented and has discounted the quality of the flock as well. Some have assumed that this new environment demands new targets, targets more related to programmatic configuration that address the cultural change, therapeutic perspectives that address the fallout in personal lives. Our fault is not that we are asking how to do church in this new and challenging context or that we are wrestling with how we heal the phenomenal brokenness that increases around us. Our fault is that we are tempted to assume that this new environment changes the target, while our new environment has simply changed the direction and velocity of the wind.[1]

The cultural context is both challenging and a source of leadership temptation. We are to minister within our culture, but not allow cultural fads, methods, or philosophy to replace the simplicity of our faith in God's Word and God's power. The Spirit of God is well able to build great churches and fruitful ministries.

The Promise Revived, Revisited, and Recovered

Sarah's delay in child-bearing was broken by

one visitation of God. Genesis 21:1-2 says that "the Lord visited Sarah as He had said, and the Lord did for Sarah as He had spoken. For Sarah conceived and bore Abraham a son in his old age, at the set time of which God had spoken."

Our churches will be fruitful as we receive our visitation of God's holy presence upon our brokenness, our unfulfillment, and our human failures. God will visit us according to His promises. He will do for us according to His Word. It will be in His timing, not ours. It will be through His miracle power, not our slick managerial leadership styles.

His breakthrough will be accompanied by a canopy of grace: people being added to the church daily, financial release, multiplication in the leadership, increased missions activity, city penetration, family restoration, and healthy signs of spiritual life.

The visitation from God upon leaders experiencing delays in their ministries is the visitation of His Holy Spirit, His fresh and powerful presence. The Scriptures speak of a reviving or a refreshing promise to the Church. The most common Old Testament word translated "revive" comes from the Hebrew verb *hayah,* which in one sense means "to be" but in another sense means to recover, repair, give new life, refresh, restore, and to make alive again.

God's Visitations, Our Preparations

Past visitations may not be indicative of future visitations. God could be up to something new. We may miss a new visitation of God if we are:

• Not open to accept the Holy Spirit moving in a fresh way because it is not according to our denominational or religious background.

• Not open, because the new way is illogical to the natural mind.

• Not moving in fresh truths because of fear that we may be identified with those who have misused or abused these same truths.

A visitation of God today upon the church:

• May only come to those who have prepared for visitation and are prayerfully anticipating it;

• May be more of a slow "adding" to the church by God's presence than by a "revival" type outpouring that comes quickly and subsides;

• May mean a cleaning up of His house, a "sweeping clean visitation," which is not popular but probable;

• May be an overwhelming sense of God's approval by His presence to those who are building by God's principles and patterns.

Psalm 65:9-13 yields eight descriptions of God's visitation:

A time of spiritual watering by the rain of
   God;

A time of enriching river;

A time of spiritual provision;

A time of soil preparation;

A time of blessing and prosperity;

A time of global ministry;

A time of sheep multiplication;

A time of rejoicing.

Faith It till You Make It

Sarah's delay in child-bearing was broken by believing in the promise. "And the Lord visited Sarah
as He had said" (Gen. 21:1). It will be our believing
in God's Word or promise by faith, not by the natural mind, that will break our delayed promises.

Romans 4:20 says, "He staggered not at the
promise of God through unbelief; but was strong in
faith, giving glory to God" (*KJV*). Abraham did not

"stagger" or "waver through unbelief." He rejected unbelief and remained faithful to God's promise. Unbelief, doubt, and staggering are all products of a barren heart (Ps. 78:19; 2 Kings 7:2).

The word "stagger" again points us toward the problem of leaning on our reasoning tendencies. To stagger means to make use of our own judgments and rationale in discerning things. To "stagger at the promise" is to take into consideration the promise and all the difficulties that lie in the way of its accomplishment and to dispute its fulfillment. Staggering is not to fully cast it off nor to fully embrace it, but to waver over it.

Unbelief focuses on our power to accomplish, fulfill, and make things happen. But depending upon our own limited resources only magnifies the problem. Unbelief is also strengthened when we focus on the natural, physical, and temporal things of life. Giving all our attention to circumstances without a faith attitude will discourage our souls. Instead, when God promises something, we must magnify His power and refer the event to His will.

The more difficult the fulfillment, the more powerful and wonderful will be our matured faith. Faith grows by going through the test, the seasons of delay and silence.

Strong faith is not antirational—it is supported by abundant reasons. All the reasons that justify our believing in God at all justify our believing in Him most firmly. He cannot lie! He is all powerful! He is God! Is anything too hard for the Lord? By having unquestioning confidence in His promises, we bring glory to God and break through the season of unfruitfulness.

Often we are brought to the end of our resources and go to pieces, like Paul's ship. Yet at the right time and in the right way, the divine Promiser fulfills His promise; the fulfillment is as certain as His own existence (Heb. 1:3, 14; 11:2; Rom. 4:20).

Just as Abraham and Sarah broke the bonds of barrenness by exercising faith in God, who always fulfills His word, so our faith can grow strong when the winds of adversity blow the hardest. Faith and patience inherit the promises of God. Let's face it! The promise will not be fulfilled without problems. Therefore you must decide now: "I will not stagger. I will not give up. I will wait for the promise."

Our attitude must be steadfast. We must have a disposition of mind that will accept the adversities and the crosses disposed to us by providence.

The Faith Attitude

A faith attitude is:

• A willingness to wait for God's timing without weariness or irksome longings for alteration, living according to these precepts: "It is good that one should hope and wait quietly for the salvation [provision] of the Lord" (Lam. 3:26). "Rest in the Lord, and wait patiently for Him" (Ps. 37:7). "Wait on the Lord; be of good courage, and He shall strengthen your heart" (Ps. 27:14);

• An entire submission and resignation of our wills to the will of God, suppressing all rebellious insurrections and grievous resentments of heart against His providence (Matt. 26:36);

• A thorough persuasion that nothing befalls us by fate or by chance or by the mere agency of inferior causes, but that all things proceed from the dispensation of or with the allowance of God (Job 2:10);

• A firm belief that all occurrences, however cross to our desires, are well consistent with the justice, wisdom, and goodness of God (Job 38:1—42:6);

• A full satisfaction of mind that all things work together for our good according to God's purpose

(Gen. 45:5; 50:20, 24; Rom. 8:28);

• Bearing delays calmly, cheerfully, and courageously in order to avoid being discomposed with anger or grief; not to be put out of humor, not to be dejected or disheartened, but in our disposition of mind to resemble the New Testament saints who "took joyfully the spoiling of [their] goods" (Heb. 10:34, KJV), and who counted it all joy when they fell into various tribulations (Jas. 1:2);

• Humility of mind wrought by our adversity, which softens our hard hearts. Humility or lowliness means to be sober in our self-understanding, sensible of our manifold defects and sins. It includes being meek and gentle, tender and pliable in our temper and frame of spirit, deeply affected with reverence and dread toward the awful majesty, mighty power, perfect justice, and complete holiness of God.

Faith in God as the Promiser

The following are some verses that are important to rest your faith upon when walking through seasons of delayed fulfillment:

Numbers 23:19: "God is not a man, that He should lie, nor a son of man, that He should repent. Has He said, and will He not do it? Or has He spoken, and will He not make it good?"

1 Kings 8:56: "Blessed be the Lord, who has given rest to His people Israel, according to all that He promised. There has not failed one word of all His good promise, which He promised through His servant Moses."

Psalm 84:11: "For the Lord God is a sun and shield; the Lord will give grace and glory; no good thing will He withhold from those who walk uprightly."

Isaiah 55:10,11: "For as the rain comes down, and the snow from heaven, and do not return there, but water the earth, and make it bring forth and bud, that it may give seed to the sower and bread to the eater, so shall My word be that goes forth from My mouth; it shall not return to Me void, but it shall accomplish what I please, and it shall prosper in the thing for which I sent it."

Hebrews 6:18: "That by two immutable things, in which it is impossible for God to lie, we might have strong consolation, who have fled for refuge to lay hold of the hope set before us."

Hebrews 10:23: "Let us hold fast the confession of our hope without wavering, for He who promised is faithful."

Lessons in Faith

In this chapter we have discovered that:

• The life of faith is built around promises given, tests encountered, and fulfillment enjoyed.

• We must all face the reasoning test as we pass

through seasons of delayed fulfillment.

• Partial truths are usually the basis for spiritual error.

• When we try to birth answers to God's promises, we find ourselves living with Ishmaels that mock our promises and make us miserable.

• Unbelief is prolific with creative schemes that delay the promise, deepen our depression, and derail our focus.

Making It Personal

1. If you are experiencing delays in your ministry vision, you have probably encountered the reasoning test. In what ways have you tried to "help" God fulfill your vision?

2. Have your efforts birthed any Ishmaels that now mock your faith and make you feel embarrassed or angry? Rather than blaming your Ishmael, what have you learned about yourself through this test?

3. Where is your focus? Are you fully convinced that God is who He says He is?

4. Will you take the challenge to memorize the verses at the end of this chapter so your faith will be anchored upon His Word?

Chapter 2

DELAYS THAT APPEAR CONTRADICTORY

My wife had been barren for several years, during which I had fasted, prayed, wept, laughed, threatened, bargained, and changed nothing. So when the Holy Spirit first asked me to pray for barren women, to move in the realm of faith for something I had no apparent success in, I'm embarrassed to reveal that my response was much like Jonah's—I didn't want to obey.

But I did as told, and months later, when I heard the news that several women had what they called "miracle babies," I was murmuring, grumbling, and discouraged because our prayers for our own child had not been answered. I wanted to find my juniper tree and call it quits. This was not a proper pastoral response to news of these miracle births.

The Contradiction Test

Contradiction. The word ruminated in my mind. For out of my emptiness others had been blessed with fruitfulness. Out of my brokenness others received wholeness. Out of my weakness others had received strength. Slowly but surely, this spiritual law of contradiction that had been in the shadows of obscurity was beginning to take on clarity. I began to see it in Scripture—first through Jesus' life, then in the lives of other biblical characters. Jesus endured contradictions with joy, stayed on course, and finished His race. Hebrews 12:3 reads, "For consider him that endured such *contradiction* of sinners against himself" (*KJV*, italics added).

To contradict is to assert the opposite of what someone has said, to speak in denial, to have someone oppose you. Most of God's servants who received a promise, vision, dream, or faith direction were tested and challenged with contradictions. Let's look at a few of them:

• Abraham and Sarah received the promise of a miracle son, but she was barren.

• Joseph dreamed of promotion and prosperity but received prison and hatred.

• Moses received a word that he would be a deliverer but was rejected and sent into the wilderness.

• David was anointed to be king but was driven into hiding by the jealousy of King Saul.

• Stephen was stoned and died. Paul was stoned and lived.

• Philip was supernaturally transported, but Paul was shipwrecked and snake-bitten.

• Peter walked on water. Paul floated in the water for three days.

• James was beheaded while Peter was released.

Our Will vs. God's Will

Contradictions in life and ministry are numerous and part of God's plan for shaping great leaders. Contradictions are our crosses to bear, and we are commanded to bear them (Matt. 16:24). A cross is made of two pieces of wood meeting and crossing each other, running contrary to each other. As we've often heard, the cross represents our thoughts crossing God's thoughts, our will crossing God's will, our desired results or answers crossing God's given answers.

God allows contradictions to enter our perfect worlds to press us, break us, and bring us to our knees. God sends contradictions to test our responses or reactions. Will we become broken or bitter? Soft or hard? Our confession changes as we embrace contradictions or the unchangeable circumstances of life: a child born with mental or physical problems; a disease that refuses to let go of a friend or loved one; an accident that takes the innocent godly person into eternity at the height of his or her life and ministry; a church that splits right after a vision meeting; a church that grows numerically, financially, and in other ways while the senior pastor is living in gross sin; at the same time, a pastor with utmost integrity plods along with few people, financial scarcity, and no recognition. Contradiction.

Contradictions, afflictions, the delay of promises, dreams, visions—this is the way of the Cross. This is the way of ministry both in unfruitful churches and in productive churches. During the contradiction test, Psalm 18:30 may be hard to confess: "As for God, His way is perfect; the word of the Lord is proven." However, once we have come through it, we can say, "Before I was afflicted I went astray, but now I keep Your word" (Ps. 119:67).

As pastors and leaders, we identify with the trial of delays and unfruitfulness because we all go through it during different seasons of our church, ministry, and personal lives. And when we go through it, what we desire simply does not happen at all or happens so slowly that we become totally discouraged.

Let me assure you, this is a test, only a test! Be encouraged with those unexplainable contradictions that loom over your life and ministry. Reinvite God into a place of fruitful activity in the face of your unfruitfulness, for "this too shall pass."

Lessons in Delayed Blessing

Rebekah, Isaac's wife, received a promise of unparalleled growth, which we read about in Genesis 24:60: "And they blessed Rebekah and said to her: 'Our sister, may you become the mother of thousands of ten thousands; and may your descendants possess the gates of those who hate them.'"

Rebekah received the promises of divine blessing, supernatural growth, and victory in warfare. Every pastor has received the same promises in the following passages:

Matthew 16:18,19: "And I also say to you that you are Peter, and on this rock I will build My church, and the gates of Hades shall not prevail against it. And I will give you the keys of the kingdom of heaven, and whatever you bind on earth will be bound in heaven, and whatever you loose on earth will be loosed in heaven."

Matthew 28:17,18: "When they saw Him, they

worshiped Him; but some doubted. And Jesus came and spoke to them, saying, 'All authority has been given to Me in heaven and on earth.'"

Luke 24:46-49: "Then He said to them, 'Thus it is written, and thus it was necessary for the Christ to suffer and to rise from the dead the third day, and that repentance and remission of sins should be preached in His name to all nations, beginning at Jerusalem. And you are witnesses of these things. Behold, I send the Promise of My Father upon you; but tarry in the city of Jerusalem until you are endued with power from on high.'"

With these promises, delay is certain. Times and seasons will arise when all you do is blanketed with emptiness rather than growth and prosperity. As leaders, pastors, and spiritual mentors, our response must be an Isaac response: "Now Isaac pleaded with the Lord for his wife, because she was barren and the Lord granted his plea. . .and Rebekah his wife conceived." Hold your promise before the Lord for your particular ministry, flock, congregation, or group. "Holding up the promise" speaks of intercessory prayer.

The Three Promises to the Unfruitful Church

Let's consider the three promises of Genesis 24:60.

1. The Promise of Divine Blessing

And they blessed Rebekah.

The Hebrew verb "to bless" (*barak*) means "to endue with power for success, prosperity, longevity, provision, protection, glory, honor, and favor." These words speak of success in everything you put your hand to do, to be raised to great honor and receive promotion (Gen. 39:3,23; Josh. 1:7; Ps. 1:3; 118:25; 122:7; 2 Chron. 26:5; 31:21).

The true blessing of God is received by those

who *trust* God and *abide* by His principles without manipulating those principles. They trust that God will give what is right and leave the timing and measure of success entirely in His hands (Mark 4:26-29; 1 Kings 3:5-15). Our prayer is for the blessing of the Lord to rest upon us. We have the assurance that "the blessing of the Lord brings wealth, and he adds no trouble to it" (Prov. 10:22, *NIV*), and that "all these blessings will come upon you and accompany you if you obey the Lord your God" (Deut. 28:2, *NIV*).

2. The Promise of Supernatural Growth

Our sister, may you become the mother of thousands and ten thousands.

This is a promise of enlargement of all areas of ministry and congregation, a new stretching that opens up windows of opportunity to receive the supernatural growth God has for you, your house, your ministry and place of spiritual service. Lord, we pray, enlarge our:

Habitation (Isa. 54:2)

Vision (1 Chron. 4:10; Prov. 29:18)

Steps (2 Sam. 22:37)

Heart (Isa. 60:5)

Borders (Exod. 34:24)

Confession (Ps. 32:1-3)

Chambers (Ezek. 41:7; Proverbs 24:3;
        2 Cor. 4:7)

Ministry (2 Cor. 6:11,13; 10:15)

The Church in America is in desperate need of supernatural church-growth breakthrough. We have organized, planned, and worked diligently to see breakthroughs in true conversion growth.

3. The Promise of Victory in Warfare

And may your descendants possess the gates of those who hate them.

To possess the gates of the enemy was to occupy the place of authority, power, and ultimate control. Biblically, gates represented the entrances of the ways leading to life and to destruction. The word "gates" then became a synonym for power because of the strength and importance of the gates to the city. Gates also represented those who held covenant and administered justice. Proverbs 8:34 says, "Blessed is the man who listens to me, watching daily at my gates, waiting at the posts of my doors." And in Proverbs 31:23 we read, "Her husband is known in the gates when he sits among the elders of the land." The elders, the spiritual authority of God's people, sat at the gates (Deut. 21:19; Ruth 4:10-11).

The promise to all leaders is that the *gates* of hell shall not prevail against the Church. All the authority, power, and evil influence of hell will not and cannot resist a restored church. Hell's gates shall pour out its hosts to assault the Church of

Christ, but the Church shall not be overcome. Hell will fortify itself against the Church, but its gates will not hold out against the Church. Instead, the Church will batter down the gates of hell. Matthew 16:18 in other translations underscores our victory in warfare:

• "And the gates of Hades will not overcome it" (*NIV*).

• "And the powers of death will never have the power to destroy it" (*Phillips*).

• "And the gates of Hades shall not overpower it [or be strong to its detriment or hold out against it]" (*AMP.*).

Rebekah received this promise long before its fulfillment. Rebekah's future was described as blessed beyond her imagination. She would break out of her physically barren condition to experience divine blessing, supernatural enlargement, and victory over her enemies.

The Isaac Response: Intercessory Prayer

One of the keys to breaking through delays is the Isaac response: "[He] pleaded with the Lord" (Gen. 25:21). The verb "pleaded" (*athar*) in this verse is one of the Hebrew words used for intercession in Scripture. H. C. Leupold translates this verse, "And Isaac interceded with Yahweh in behalf of his wife, for she was childless, and Yahweh granted his entreaty and Rebekah his wife conceived."[2]

It is interesting to note that Isaac is the only patriarch whose intercession is recorded up to that point in Scripture. His prayer was for this unusual moment. He was concerned with the promised seed. This is the second time the wife of one who perpetuates the line of promise was barren and the childlessness was, in God's time, remedied. In Rebekah's situation, it is intercessory prayer – Isaac standing in the gap for his wife – that broke the delay in her child-bearing. Conception or the absence of conception is more directly due to the omnipotent power of the Creator than people are ready to believe.

Intercessory prayer is intensified praying, which involves three special ingredients:

1. Identification of the intercessor with the one who is interceded for.

2. Agony to feel the burden, the pain, the suffering, the need.

3. Authority that is the gained position of the intercessor to speak with authority that sees results.[3]

Isaac moved into gap-standing for his wife. This is the Ezekiel 22:30 intercession: "So I sought for a man among them who would make a wall, and stand in the gap before Me on behalf of the land, that I should not destroy it; but I found no one." In Luke 1:13, Zacharias also interceded for his barren wife, and God answered his prayers: "But the angel said to him, 'Do not be afraid, Zacharias, for your prayer is heard; and your wife Elizabeth will bear you a son, and you shall call his name John.'"

May God open our eyes to see what the holy ministry of intercession is that we, as leaders who face delayed promises, may use powerfully. We have been set apart to exercise the ministry of intercession. May He give us a large and strong heart to believe the mighty influence our prayers can have so that we may echo the words of Job: "But as for me, I would seek God, and to God I would commit my cause, who does great things, and unsearchable, marvelous things without number" (Job 5:8, 9).

Stop, Seek, and See

The Isaac response could be a model example for all leaders going through waiting seasons—it is the "stop, seek, and see" model.

Stop. Busyness is not the answer.

Seek His face. Focus, not on the delayed promise, but on the God who can break the bonds or give you insight and grace to handle it. Wait upon His timing. *See* His answers. He alone is able to fulfill His promises.

The two main Hebrew words used for seeking the Lord are (1) *darash,* meaning "to tread; to frequent; to follow hard after as a pursuer for pursuit or search; to seek; to ask; to make diligent inquiry; to desire something deeply" and (2) *baqash,* meaning "to seek to find; seek to secure; seek the face of; desire; require; or request." He who desires not from the depths of his heart makes a deceptive prayer. Intercessory prayer that breaks seasons of unfruitfulness begins with a seeking heart.

The following are verses to meditate upon as you seek His face:

Deut. 4:29: "But from there you will *seek* the Lord your God, and you will find Him if you seek

Him with all your heart and with all your soul."

1 Chron. 16:10: "Glory in His holy name; let the hearts of those rejoice who seek the Lord!"

1 Chron. 16:11: "Seek the Lord and His strength; *seek* His face evermore!"

1 Chron. 22:19: "Now set your heart and your soul to *seek* the Lord your God. Therefore arise and build the sanctuary of the Lord God, to bring the ark of the covenant of the Lord and the holy articles of God into the house that is to be built for the name of the Lord."

2 Chron. 11:16: "And after the Levites left, those from all the tribes of Israel, such as set their heart to seek the Lord God of Israel, came to Jerusalem to sacrifice to the Lord God of their fathers."

Job 5:8: "But as for me, I would seek God, and to God I would commit my cause."

Ps. 27:8: "When You said, 'Seek My face,' my heart said to You, 'Your face, Lord, I will seek.'"

Dan. 9:3: "And I set my face unto the Lord God, to seek by prayer and supplications, with fasting, and sackcloth, and ashes" (*KJV*).

Lessons in Contradictions

In this chapter we have discovered that:

• Those who receive a promise, dream, vision, or faith direction can expect to encounter the contradiction test.

• God sends contradictions to test our responses and reactions. Will we become broken or bitter?

• Even in our unfulfilled state, we are promised divine blessing, supernatural growth, and victory in warfare.

• If we want to be faith giants, we must do so without manipulating His principles and we must leave the timing and measure of success entirely to Him.

• Intercessory prayer requires identification

with the one who is interceded for, agony to feel the burden, and authority in Christ.

• We must stop our busyness in order to seek His face so we can see His answers.

Making It Personal

1. What are some of the contradictory places you are walking through right now? Is God asking you to give to others out of your emptiness?

2. Who is God asking you to intercede for as you face your contradiction test?

3. Is busyness preventing you from hearing God's voice? What is your fear? Where is your focus?

4. Are you prepared to adopt God's timetable for breakthrough? Are you willing to be content with His measure of success?

Chapter 3

DELAYS DUE TO
WRONG ATTITUDES

$\mathcal{I}$t is easy to see why God would have compassion for Leah, the less-loved wife of Jacob. Jacob's love for his other wife Rachel was based largely upon her physical attractiveness, leaving Leah feeling rejected by her husband as well as sorrowful that she had given Jacob no children.

The Lord had sympathy for Leah: *"When the Lord saw that Leah was unloved, He opened her womb"*

(Gen. 29:31). Blessed by God, Leah gave birth in the following years to a daughter and four sons—all of whom were significant in the history of Israel.

The Lack of Love

The lessons in delayed promises from Leah and Jacob are rich and many. Leah may represent churches ministered to by leaders without deep, godly love for their churches. Maybe for the leader it was the only church open at that time, or a way to get through seminary, or perhaps an opportunity to gain experience. All were selfish reasons, lacking the genuine call of God and the heart of a true loving shepherd.

Most leaders do not strategically plan to be hirelings or unloving shepherds, but the enemy of our souls and the flock will take advantage of these seemingly normal procedures to bring his hideous destruction to both leader and flock. A fastidious preacher was challenged by a layman because he boasted of his qualifications. The layman said, "Why see now, without your gown you dare not preach, without your book you could not preach, without your pay you would not preach!"[4]

God will take notice of any congregation that is experiencing unfruitfulness due to a lack of love from the leadership. When a church or ministry is not fruitful, the temptation of the leader is to refuse to deeply love the people. This lack of true pastoral/ leadership compassion is felt by the congregation and will cause deep spiritual wounds. Loving the growth, numbers, finance, building, and influence more than the people is a grievous and gross error.

Negativity, a Foundation for Delays

When leaders dislike the church, they have usually cultivated an attitude of negativity toward their city, toward their people, and toward the church building itself. Negativity is a habitual bias toward grumbling, murmuring, complaining, and being pessimistic about everyone and anything. The bent toward negativity usually spirals downward, affecting everyone around. People given to negativism have usually lost the spirit of joy, their sense of humor, and their passion for life, family, and ministry.

When a pastor or leader becomes a strongly negative person, everything around that person's sphere of influence is polluted. When the church is the recipient of this attitude, the atmosphere of the church becomes unhealthy, unhappy, and unproductive. A negative attitude, if not the main source, is a great contributing factor to delays in spiritual fruitfulness.

The flaws become the focus in a Leah church: The church is not located in the right city. The building is inadequate; the technology is a hundred years behind; there is no parking; the lighting is poor; the pews are uncomfortable; the audio system squeals and sounds demonically harassed; the pulpit is too short; and the people are not what could be called a quality congregation. The salary is nonnegotiable and painfully low. The leadership board members are all related and have been there for decades. This is not the best choice of a church.

Negative attitudes are cultivated. Initially, only the hidden thoughts of comparison with other ministries or churches are detected; then a few lighthearted comments begin to surface. Eventually an all-out negative thought pattern infected with continual negative and sarcastic comments dominates all that is said and done. It's hard to hide: You don't love them, and they don't love you. Negativity has found root in both pastor and flock. This is a spiritual stronghold that must be weeded out immediately. In order to uproot, tear down, and pull out this diabolical attitude, let's look at its causes and cures:

• Negativity is easily nurtured in a person who has lost the spirit of expectation for anything good to happen.

• Negativity is usually experienced by a person who has slowly lost the attitude of appreciation for not only the little things in life, but also family, ministry, or church.

• Negativity is a stronghold in the mind that Satan takes advantage of, causing depression, fear, doubt, and worry.

• Negativity can be defeated by developing honesty in facing the present problem, repenting for the lack of pastoral love for God's people, and publicly beginning to make statements of hope, forgiveness, expectation, faith, and appreciation.

• Negativity can be defeated as we build altars of rejoicing and take time to build memories of God's goodness.

Is it possible for ministers to hate their churches and love their ministries? Is it possible for ministers to build expectations of churches because of books, seminars, magazines, internet information, and other forms of communication that exalt numbers, growth, and influence? Does it really surprise us that so many churches lose pastors every two to three years solely because their Leahs do not fulfill them any longer and they are searching for their Rachels?

If It's Not Unconditional, It's Not Love

As leaders, we must all learn to give unconditional love and deep compassion to the churches we serve, despite the lack of spiritual growth. Could it be our lack of true love for our congregations is one of the bonds that limits our fruitfulness? Leah thirsted for the love denied her by Jacob. Only by the sovereign grace and compassion of God was she able to find that love as God opened her womb.

Joseph M. Stowell in his book *Shepherding the Church into the Twenty-First Century* addresses the necessity of a leader loving the church:

Love is at the heart of what it means to be a shepherd. Shepherds are caring, flock-focused individuals whose primary motivation is not the interest of self but the interest of the safety, security, and satisfaction of the flock. Given this, a discussion of love in terms of the shepherd's ministry is of great importance. And it must be more than a discussion. It must lead to a commitment that transcends the circumstances of the shepherd's life or the configuration of the shepherd's congregation.[5]

The heart of true ministry is a heart of unconditional love for God and His people. The philosopher Rousseau is purported to have said, "The more I get to know people, the more I love my dog." This attitude may be the product of a few bad days with the flock, but withdrawing and becoming cynical, hardened, or heartlessly professional is unacceptable to both God and His people.

If you desire a Leah church, a church that pleads with God for productivity in order to please the husband/pastor, then lead without love and you will have it. We must love God's people without any need to be rewarded by them, without any need to find our fulfillment in their success or achievement (John 3:16; Rom. 5:8).

Church history is replete with heartbreaking, tragic stories of leaders whose focus was dedicated to using and abusing the Church for the benefit of their own needs and desires. These leaders have battered the spirit of the Church, scattered people to the four corners of the earth and damaged the testimony of Christ (Jer. 23:1-4).

Leaders must give of themselves freely and completely, without reserving a part for something else or being concerned about the reward for such sacrifice. Those who choose to be passionate in their love for God's people will find God rewarding them, abundantly above all that they could ever imagine, in His way and in His time. Let it not be said, "And the Lord saw that Leah was unloved." Barrenness can be turned to awesome growth through the love of God and the love of God's leaders.

Let your Leah church feel your love, your passion, and your satisfaction! Decide in your heart that the words of Jeremiah 23:4 will be spoken of you: "'I will set up shepherds over them who will feed them; and they shall fear no more, nor be dismayed, nor shall they be lacking,' says the Lord."

Developing a Mature Attitude

You can have a mature attitude. You can become the leader God wants you to be. Your attitude can help to break through the delay in promised blessings. You can raise up a Kingdom standard of loving leadership that will bring earthly and eternal rewards. What does a mature attitude look like? It is:

• An attitude of restraining your tongue from all complaints, discontent, and murmurings; restraining from all profane, harsh expressions, importing displeasure or dissatisfaction in God's dealings toward you; arguing desperation or distrust in Him.

• An attitude of blessing and praising God, declaring your hearty satisfaction in God's proceedings with you, acknowledging and expressing gratefulness for His wisdom, justice, and goodness therein; maintaining this attitude in conformity to Job who, upon the loss of all his comforts, did thus vent his mind: "The Lord gave, and the Lord has taken away; blessed be the name of the Lord" (Job 1:21).

• An attitude of abstaining from all irregular and unworthy courses toward the removal or redress of your crosses, choosing to abide quietly under their pressure rather than to relieve or relax yourself by any unwarrantable means.

• An attitude of fair behavior toward the instruments of your affliction—those who brought you into it or who detain you under it by withholding relief or refusing to yield the help that you might expect; having the forbearance to express any wrath or displeasure, to exercise any revenge, to retain any grudge or enmity toward those people, but rather, even on that score, bearing good will, and showing kindness to them.

• An attitude of patience toward those who, by injurious and offensive language, provoke you so that you (1) will not be easily, immoderately, or perniciously incensed with anger toward them; (2) do not harbor any ill will, ill wishes, or ill designs toward them, but truly desire their good and intend to further it as you have ability and occasion; (3) do not execute any revenge or do any mischief to them for revenge, either in word or deed.

Should a God who laid down His life for His Bride expect any less from those who are called to care for her until His return?

Lessons in Attitude

In this chapter we have discovered that:

• God takes notice of people who are experiencing a lack of love from ministry leaders.

• Lovelessness produces negativity, which can result in delayed fulfillment.

• Negativity is a habitual bias toward grumbling, murmuring, complaining, and being pessimistic.

• Lack of positive expectation, heartfelt gratitude, and wholehearted forgiveness are all signs of a negative attitude.

• The heart of true ministry is one of unconditional love for God and His people.

• A mature attitude is grateful in spite of loss, forgiving in spite of persecution, and patient in spite of unyielding circumstances.

Making It Personal

1. What is your real motive for ministry?

2. Are you the leader of a Leah or a Rachel? Has your ministry been the victim of a fraudulent expectation, or are you willing to sacrifice all for your Leah?

3. Is your heart "flock focused" or "reward focused"? In what ways do you need to change?

4. What are some of the negative attitudes the Holy Spirit wants to improve in you?

Chapter 4

DELAYS DUE TO ENVY

$\mathscr{I}$ don't know which is worse: feeling the undeniable emotion of envy or jealousy toward a fellow minister, or becoming the target of jealousy from other ministers. Envy is not an easy emotion or mindset to admit or keep under wraps once it starts, but one conclusion is certain: Everyone deals with this subtle enemy in life, in church, and in the ministry.

Envy comes with varying degrees of potency.

A little spark of jealousy seems easily conquered when need be. It comes, it goes, and it seldom lingers: just a hot rush once in a while or a shadow of an envious thought, a jealous daydream. Maybe it is a logical proposition of another's worth and a quick judgment of that person such as, *He doesn't deserve it. It's not fair. He is probably compromising something else in order to have that.* Envy may be felt about a golf swing, an expensive home, car, jewelry, or someone's ministry or church. But make no mistake—envy is cruel, destructive, and swift. Its embittering flame consumes character and destroys the bloom of beauty.

Releasing Envy

The Holy Spirit penetrates our hearts when we least expect it and sometimes least desire it. The word impressed upon my mind was unwelcome and, I felt, unwarranted: Envier. Frank, you are envying that ministry. You're jealous. You must give it up!

"Envier." I better check my dictionary and study this, I thought. That's a safe response to a direct hit by the Holy Spirit. Let me see, envied, envier, envious, enviously, envy. An envier is "one who envies another; one who desires what another possesses and hates him because his condition is better than his own or wishes his downfall."[6] Well, that's certainly descriptive of someone driven by carnal impulses. At first I assumed the Holy Spirit was asking me to assist in bringing deliverance to other leaders bound by this spiritual disease. Then I realized, no, that's not the case—it's me! It's my spirit that has allowed an envious jealousy to take root. How could I have done that?

To be envious is to have a feeling of uneasiness around the person envied. This harbored feeling of envy is aroused when surveying the excellence, prosperity, or happiness of another. You know this feeling when you are pained by the desire of possessing some superior thing that another already possesses. With envy come other emotions: rivalry, comparison, malice, grudges, and criticism. Like a baseball runner who has been trapped between bases, I was trapped. I didn't know which way to run, so I gave up, surrendered, laid down my excuses, admitted my sin, and asked for cleansing.

Envy in the ministry cannot be tolerated. It has been the demise of many great leaders and the pollution of many pure wells. Envy—the pain, the uneasiness, or discontent excited by the sight of another's superiority or success—is accompanied by some degree of hatred or malignity and often a desire or an effort to depreciate the other person or to take pleasure in seeing that person depressed. Envy springs from pride, ambition, or jealousy that another has obtained what one has a strong desire to possess (Job 5:2; Prov. 3:31; 14:30; 23:17; 27:4;

Eccl. 9:6; Acts 7:9; Rom. 1:29; Phil. 1:15; 1 Tim. 6:4; Titus 3:3; Jas. 4:5). In Scripture, envy and jealousy are usually accompanied by murder, strife, deceit, malice, and other ills that bring rottenness to the soul.

I considered my jealousy innocent. His church was bigger. His buildings were nicer. His location was perfect. He had the worship leader I needed, the musicians I dreamed of. The cool people in town attended his church: the wealthy, the young, the influential. He had a better radio time and a better television spot. He had the car I would like to have driven, but I was too wise and too humble! He lived where we longed to build our retirement dream home. He golfed better. Every time I got a brochure about a conference I wanted to attend, he was already attending—as the speaker!

Jealous. Envious. These two words are interchangeable—they both stem from an unhealthy need to compare. I was in the "unfruitful" category, and he was in the "blessed and growing without any effort" category. I found myself thinking, *If only I could be successful in all the same ways, I would then be fulfilled!*

Envy Within the Church

The words in Genesis 30:1-2 leaped off the page and right into my life experience. They mirrored my feelings exactly: "Now when Rachel saw that she bore Jacob no children, Rachel envied her sister, and said to Jacob, 'Give me children, or else I die.'"

That's it! That's my heart and my dilemma, I thought. I have envied the Leah church for bearing children, for being fruitful, for finding and enjoying success. Without realizing it, my passion had become twisted: "Give me children, lest I die. Give me growth, success, influence, or else I shall die." Not die physically, but my vision, my faith, my joy, my passions would die. Without results in the ministry, surely something would have to die, so my prayer was, "Give me, lest I die."

This insatiable appetite for producing is one of the subtle traps of ministry fulfillment and success. In ministry, success can be spelled in larger attendance numbers, better programs, more popular people, bigger buildings, and a sense of celebrity around the pastors. Fulfillment is perceived as one of life's choicest gifts, a major building block toward authentic ministry and authentic fruitfulness. Rachel pastors cry, "Give me fulfillment, lest I die." But as we see in Scripture, the Rachel cry of the heart would be tempered by the dealings of God. God would give to Leah four sons before He would begin to move on behalf of barren Rachel.

The unfruitful Rachel churches may be small in number or large in number, have massive buildings, properties, and moneys or be of lesser stature. Size and money are not the issue. The Rachel church is driven by the inability to reach the ultimate edge of vision.

The Sovereignty of God

Rachel was the fourth wife of a patriarch to suffer a season of barrenness. God was making it very apparent that human ambitions and human services were not to carry on the line of promise and furnish the desired offspring. Rachel was the favored wife of Jacob. She was beautiful in every way. She had everything a young wife could desire, everything but the blessing of children—the one thing she could not use her beauty to influence or acquire.

Rachel was trapped by the sovereignty of God's plans and purposes. Her jealousy was unacceptable, inexcusable, and her impatient carnality caused harmful results. Rachel, in her angry, jealous state, questioned the wisdom of God and demanded from

Jacob what he could not give to break her barren-ness. Rachel threatened Jacob with her unreason-able demand, "Give me children, lest I die."

Jacob's response to Rachel's jealous anger is un-derstandable:

And Jacob's anger was aroused against Rachel, and he said, "Am I in the place of God, who has withheld from you the fruit of the womb?" (Gen. 30:2).

He knew he could not stand in God's place as the source of divine plans, changing people, rul-ing over the womb of the barren or providing the miracle of conception. Jacob understood that both fruitfulness and its absence are under the divine will and control of—not man or woman—but God Himself.

The lessons of patience, faith, submission to God's sovereign ways and means are offered in the stories of all four patriarchal wives. From them, we learn that jealousy and envy will only delay the desired blessings of God upon our ministries and our churches. Whatever attitudes or spirit we allow to become dominant in our lives and ministries will be passed on to our congregations.

In his book *Pastors of Promise*, Jack Hayford states, "I saw that whatever 'spirit' governs me at any point or practice will determine the mood, life, and practice of the whole congregation. As a result of that pivotal encounter, I learned a crucial lesson and during my years of ministry I have noticed a general principle. It may not explain all church problems, but I am convinced that many conflicts within congregations are but the sad projection of a pastor's own lack of submission to some aspect of God's will in his own life."[7]

Delayed Blessings May Provoke Jealousy

Out of brokenness and the inability to change

or control the circumstances, a person may begin to envy and become deeply jealous of other ministers or churches. Jealousy burns like fire (Ps. 79:5) and is the rage of man (Prov. 6:34). Jealousy is as cruel as the grave (S. of S. 8:6). This embittering fire will scorch all who touch it, consume character, and destroy the potential for true spiritual fruitfulness.

Ministers or leaders experiencing seasons of drought have more pull toward this fire of jealousy, continually weighing themselves on the success scales and found wanting. However, jealousy does not always have a negative connotation.

The Bible describes jealousy in two ways: good and bad. The fire that burns in the Rachel church or barren Jacob leaders can be the fire of God instead of the fire of jealousy. Good jealousy is referred to in Exodus 20:5: "For I the Lord thy God am a jealous God," and in 2 Corinthians 11:1-2 when Paul said, "Would to God ye could bear with me a little

. . . for I am jealous over you with godly jealousy"
(*KJV*). The God kind of jealousy is a zeal of love and
of right perspective, not a self-love, but a devotion
at white heat.

Leaders must never feed on others' failures,
weaknesses, or destructions. We must keep watch
over our emotions and be introspective about our
motives. For example, when we hear the praise of
our envied one, do we become coldly silent? If that
person is criticized, do we become secretly glad?
If that person is exalted, do we praise God for the
blessing, or do we secretly murmur, mutter, and
generally nurture a bad attitude for days?

Jealousy is among the most subtle and potent
weapons in Satan's arsenal. A famous fable tells of
the devil crossing the Libyan desert where he encountered a group of fiends who were tempting a
holy hermit. They tried him with the seductions of
the flesh; they sought to sour his mind with doubt

and fears; they told him that all his austerities were worth nothing. It was of no avail. The holy man was immovable. Then the devil stepped forward. Addressing the imps he said, "Your methods are too crude. Permit me for one moment. This is what I would recommend." Going to the hermit he said, "Have you heard the news? Your brother has been made the Bishop of Alexandria." At these words, a scowl of malevolent jealousy clouded the serene face of the holy man.[8]

Have you been scowling lately? To break through her childless season, Rachel had to be set free from the hellish jealousy that was ruining her life and her future. Are you receiving instruction for your unfruitful ministry or church? Is there a Leah church or a Leah ministry that torments your soul every time you hear, see, or think of it? Is there a Leah worship leader or song writer whose blessings tighten the emptiness around your soul because of your jealousy? This diabolical emotion must be dealt with.

Jealousy distorts our personalities, ruins our characters, and floods our souls with hell's torment. It leaves us with heavy hearts, pale and palsied, and with lean souls. The soul burning with jealousy will nurse deceptive delusions, overlook the good in other ministries, refrain from celebrating and rejoicing with others, and lack the joy for living (Jas. 3:16).

A perfect illustration of jealousy's perilous prongs has been preserved in the arena chapel in Padua, where the pioneer of fresco painting, Giotto, has given allegorical representations of the deadly vices and their opposite virtues on opposing walls. Envy is a female figure who has long, wide ears to catch every breath of rumor that may hurt a neighbor's reputation; out of her mouth issues a serpent's tongue that is swift to poison all things sweet and tender. This serpent coils back on itself and stings the eyes of the envious one to blindness and the figure stands in flames, representing the fierce fire that consumes the heart that takes pleasure in others' injuries and is made bitter by their prosperity.[9]

Delays and God's Sovereignty

The church or ministry in a season of drought or delayed fulfillment may well look to the pastor or leader to bring about the miracles needed to experience fruitfulness, as we saw when Rachel cried out for relief from Jacob (Gen. 30:1-2). Churches may hire what appears to be the perfect leader to release growth, prosperity, and fulfilled vision. This may well turn into a disappointing journey for the elder board, deacon board, or whatever leadership team has hired the new pastor. The problem: The new pastor is not God!

The new pastor faced with the challenge of an older, aging, traditional church may look like the messiah of new hope and future in the board meeting, but in fact is just a human being with a gift. This distortion of focus lays an enormous amount of pressure on the pastor to produce and "give us children." This is especially true when the church has been barren for 10, 20, 30, or 100 years, and the Leah church just down the street is very productive. "Give us children, lest we die!" is a passionate cry that can ignite prayer intercession or become the threat of a carnally driven, selfish motivation.

Jacob's answer to Rachel is the only answer we pastors may give: "I'm not standing in the place of God." There is a God in heaven who is sovereign and His ways and thoughts are higher than ours (Isa. 55:10-11). He is the God who has wisdom and might, and He changes the times and seasons. He removes kings and raises up kings. He gives wisdom to the wise and knowledge to scholars (Dan. 2:20-21).

Our God is not seeking counsel from man and

does not feel any pressure to hurry His plans and purposes. He does according to His will in the army of heaven and among the inhabitants of the earth and none can stop His hands or say to Him, what are you doing? (Dan. 4:35). "Can I not do with you as this potter?" He asked of Israel in Jeremiah 18:6. God claimed to have the same absolute power over the nation as the potter exercised over the clay. In Isaiah 64:8, the potter is also our Father.

God is not an indulgent father who gives His children whatever they desire whenever they want it, irrespective of moral and spiritual considerations. We leaders are *not* responsible for producing the power of new life in order to release blessings. We *are* responsible for positioning our churches and ministries in spirit, in faith, in heart attitude and with eyes focused on an awesome God. We position, God provides and produces.

And yet we are in a hurry to vindicate our ministries and our reputations in order to bring revival or new life to our churches. We are always in a hurry to have our desires granted, but God refuses to be stampeded into premature action. Our impatience is the outcome of dealing with unproductive churches, communities, and ministries without being soaked in intercessory prayer and a huge dose of spiritual knowledge concerning God's sovereignty.

When God chooses to allow unfruitfulness for a season, He is working according to His perfect plans. Our frenzied reaction to God's seeming slowness is only a reaction of desire for His full knowledge and perfect control of every circumstance that arises in our lives. We may complain in an hour of deep distress, "God, why don't you do something? I can't take any more waiting!"

We often feel as if God has left us. However, even though Rachel and Jacob could not see God standing amid the shadows, disclosing His presence and plans, He was there with His unerring hand, never losing hold of the reins. Yes, at times God seems to hide Himself (Isa. 45:15), but God is always present, a very present help in times of trouble (Ps. 46:1-4).

Genesis 30:22 reads, "Then God remembered Rachel, and God listened to her and opened her womb." The waiting ended when the timing of God was perfect. God had completed a work in Rachel that no other test could have performed. In the fullness of time, new life burst forth and Rachel was first to give praise.

H. C. Leupold states, "Quite humbly Rachel, who early in her marriage may have been a more or less haughty and self-sufficient personage, now gives God the glory and rejoices that He has taken away her reproach. Sterility brought reproach as though God had deemed a wife unworthy of children. Rachel still stands on the lower level of faith when she makes this remark, for she thinks only of the sovereign power of God. Yet her experience of divine help raises her faith to the higher level when she asks for grace from the faithful covenant God Yahweh."[10]

Rachel's testimony recorded in Genesis 30:22-24 was:

God in His time hearkened to my voice; God in His mercy has taken away my reproach; God has added to my life what was indeed impossible; God has used my barrenness as a lesson in brokenness.

The lesson of jealousy and sovereignty brought about increased faithfulness, a greater love and dependence upon God, a purified heart, an overflowing sense of joy, a deep-seated peace, long-suffering, and a renewed sense of worship. Rachel reaped not only the fruit of the womb but also the fruit of the Spirit.

If God is delaying fulfillment in your life today, it is only to deepen the level of your fruitfulness for tomorrow.

Lessons in Comparisons

In this chapter we have discovered that:

• Envy is accompanied by some degree of hatred or malice and desires the depreciation of another human being.

• Envy can be traced to areas where we compare ourselves with others and can delay our fulfillment until we turn our eyes back to God.

• The lessons of patience, faith, and submission are taught in the waiting room.

• The attitude that dominates the leader will infiltrate the ministry.

• Leaders position the ministry; God provides and produces the spiritual growth.

Making It Personal

1. Has the Holy Spirit used this chapter to spotlight areas where you have fallen into the comparison trap of envy?

2. In what areas of your church, ministry, or personal life are you striving to fulfill a promise that only God can birth?

3. What are some of the attitudes that most concern you about your congregation, staff, or even family that you know have filtered down through your own undealt-with stuff? Do you want to be changed?

4. Have you been feeding on others' failures or weaknesses? Do you really want to see your neighbor's ministry grow, even beyond your own? If not, will you say yes to a season of unfulfillment so God can bring forth a greater harvest in you later?

Chapter 5

DELAYS TO EXPOSE OWNERSHIP

*A*s I crumbled the Styrofoam cup in my hand I said out loud, "Thank you, cup, for your willingness to be used. Now, to your destiny—crunch, into the garbage can." The destiny of that cup had been determined by its purpose, and I had desired the coffee, not the Styrofoam cup. The cup had served its purpose as a coffee-carrying vessel, and I wasn't praying or asking for any kind of a *rhema* word about Styrofoam cups when God spoke, not audibly, but by a sure Holy Spirit impression upon my inner man, a clear inner voice.

"But we have this treasure in earthen vessels, that the excellence of the power may be of God and not of us" (2 Cor. 4:7).

I paused, locking my mind for a few moments as I considered this quickened verse, *We have treasure in earthen vessels*. God then simply impressed a word upon me in a flash, a direct hit, right to the hidden parts of my heart: *Ownership. You must give up ownership*. My heart immediately responded, knowing God was using my innocent cup experience to reveal something in my life. My response was, "Father God, thank You for bringing this to my attention and for removing this from my life. Thank you."

That was the end of my divine encounter, but only the beginning of the journey to fulfill my prayer. I had naively believed a simple prayer would deliver me from this not-so-simple problem: ownership. I didn't fully understand what God was after. I had always given God my best, given Him praise for our successes. I had not tried to own anything in our ministry or church. Throughout the next several years all this would change: our ministry, our church, our future, and our rights to certain things.

Lord, Is That Really You?

I was in my car on my way to deliver a decision I had made about my future. The decision was monumental in the direction our ministries would take. The presence of God invaded my car. It was definitely real and I wasn't expecting it. The Lord's voice to me in that instant was staggering, *Lay your vision down and serve another's.*

Some might stumble at my use of the Lord's voice at a very precarious time in my life and ministry. Should a leader put that much stock in a spiritual experience, a spiritual "heavy" of an inner voice?

I'm not really given to subjective experiences such as voices, dreams, and impressions. I believe the Holy Spirit can and does speak to people and that God speaks to me. But encounters of this magnitude have only occurred a few times in my Christian life. This was a "life directional" word. Our vision had been set. How could I lay it down? It was a great vision, and God had given me the inspiration. Why should I lay it down? We had mapped out our state with a church-planting strategy. Sixty-seven places would be targeted and we were on our way to fulfilling the vision. Now came a word to stop—and even more astonishing—to serve someone else's vision.

This was my first encounter with God's secret ways and means committee to remove my tight grip on my vision, my ministry, and my future. Ownership was now becoming an issue I could identify, but still not connect to my simple prayer, "God, thank You for bringing this to my attention and for removing it from my life." God had my attention now and God had His intention: remove ownership from my spirit.

I obeyed the Lord that day, first in my car at the side of the road, weeping, praying, having a spiritual visitation. I had no human idea of what that day in my car meant, no idea that my giving up ownership of our church vision would actually seal my destiny to a future that only God could put together.

The Most Difficult Sunday of Our Journey

As I stood before our congregation, our beloved church that we had planted, nurtured, and loved with everything we had, I prepared to announce the news. We were resigning as pastors and moving back to Portland to succeed the pastor of our mother church. I had on several occasions stated my lifetime commitment, and now we were leaving. It was the most difficult and emotional decision of my adult life. I was, we were, giving up our success, the fruit of our labor, and our identity. We owned this vision. Our fingerprints were everywhere, our own unique markings.

My Styrofoam cup encounter was now making sense to me, and I didn't like it. Yes, I did pray that simple "do whatever it takes, go ahead, root out the ownership attitude in my life" prayer. But this was more than I bargained for! The church had not been my product, but God's. The church we planted had grown by God's grace, God-empowered preaching, teaching, counseling, and vision casting. This church had been God's child, a God seed, a God giving of life. I thought I knew that! The words of 1 Corinthians 3:5-7 echoed in my mind:

Who then is Paul, and who is Apollos, but ministers through whom you believed, as the Lord gave to each one? I planted, Apollos watered, but God gave the increase. So then neither he who plants is anything, nor he who waters, but God who gives the increase.

Removing Our Grip

When no human possibility exists for growth or success, we usually turn to God easily, giving Him all ownership of our ministries and churches. But when leaders are able to produce through their unique giftings, abilities, personalities, methods, and creativity, there is a certain sense of *It's mine. I gave my life and I deserve recognition, reward, and respect. I bought it, paid for it, and I own it.*

Delayed fulfillment is God's method for exposing and removing our grip, our tightfisted attitude of ownership in order to move us into a new realm of ministry. A season of drought allows us to exhaust ourselves, come to the end of fleshly carnal ambitions, and move us into the supernatural realm. After all, "we have this treasure in earthen vessels, that the excellence of the power may be of

God and not of us." We are dependent upon God's grace for new life in our ministries and churches.

The New English Bible translates 2 Corinthians 4:7 this way: "We are no better than pots of earthenware to contain this treasure, and this proves that such transcendent power does not come from us, but is God's alone."

Or as Charles Stanley states in *The Blessings of Brokenness*: "Which would you rather be? A vessel of your own design, based upon your finite mind and limited creativity, power, and wisdom—a vessel of limited use and passing value? Or a vessel of His design, based upon His infinite wisdom, love, and power—a vessel of unlimited use and eternal, unsearchable value?"[11]

Vessels of Purpose

Three women in Scripture well illustrate the point of giving up ownership—all were vessels containing a treasure. These women were brought to a place where they could, with conviction, say, "If you break my barrenness, I will give you the child. You name him. You use him. You take ownership of him." It was the pain, suffering, and dying to self that caused Manoah's wife to give up Samson, Hannah to give up Samuel, and Elizabeth to give up John the Baptist. Unfruitfulness aids us in realizing our source of success and allows God's blessings, miracles, and purposes to flow through us in His perfect timing.

Manoah's wife, Hannah, and Elizabeth all produced world-class leaders who stood in times of spiritual and historical transition. They stood at the intersections of history where the circumstances merited a bona fide miracle through the messenger of God. Each one paid a high price to offer up to the world a deliverer, a prophet-judge, and a prophet-forerunner. These women suffered for the purposes of God to be fulfilled at the divine moment. The test was pressed upon them and they grew strong in spirit; they matured in character.

Manoah's Wife: The Mother of Samson

A short glimpse of Samson's mother and the life of Samson are found in Judges 13-16. Jephthah, a leader raised up by God, was delivering the tribes on the east of the Jordan from the oppression of the Ammonites. The Philistine oppression on the west side of Jordan had gone on for 40 years. God would provide a new deliverer named Samson. Samson would appear in the fullness of time with a supernatural strength to deliver Israel from the Philistines. Samson was a miracle child, his mother a woman whose hope was in the mercy of God.

Manoah and his wife had no way to properly comprehend the enormous task their son would be called to. He would be nationally famous. Through-out the history of humanity, their son would be known and remembered as a man with supernatural strength.

Manoah's wife appeared to be just another unfortunate woman in Israel—another childless mother. While her husband's name is preserved, she remains nameless in the Bible, although the Talmud says she bore the name of Hazelelponi or Zelelponi and that she was of the tribe of Judah. Zelelponi means "the shadow fell on me," and Manoah's wife was certainly one who dwelt under the shadow of the Almighty.

Manoah's wife would receive a gift, a miracle that would change the destiny of all Israel and usher in the era of freedom all Israel dreamed about.

God's gifts to us are usually regulated in their extent by our capacity for receiving them. Manoah's wife had a receptive heart and believed the promises of God to her. In time, her prayers were answered. She understood God's ruling throughout her barren years and rejoiced in the gift of leadership granted through her son, Samson.

The Samson Dilemma

Samson's name (Hebrew: *Shimshown*) was tied to the strength and power of God, his name meaning "the strength of the sun" (Hebrew: *Shemesh*; Ps. 19:5-6; 84:11). He was to rule Israel as a delivering judge for 20 years, but not without compromise, sinful behavior, and blatant disobedience to God's laws and ways.

Samson's sinful patterns and weakness for seductive women caused great sorrow and deep disappointment to his mother. She had prayed for this savior of Israel for years and now her answered prayer failed to produce the result she had hoped for. She could not control Samson's power. His power had been given by God, yet could be used for his own pleasures. This was confusing and disappointing, not only to Samson's parents but also to Israel.

In the same way, a season of unfruitfulness may be removed from our ministries or churches by a divine act of God's favor and grace. But what we don't know is what success will do once it has been birthed. What will power do once it has been given life? Samson represents anointing unleashed, power released, and manifestation of the awesome strength of God revealed.

All ministries and churches welcome a visitation of God's miraculous power. Some are desperately waiting for God to show up. The cry for more power, more miracles, a more awesome working of God can be heard around the world. The question is, what happens when strength and miracles are birthed, honored, and released? Can we handle the authority and power of God, or will it pervert us, change us, and ultimately destroy us?

Samson: a New Power, a New Test

Samson killed a lion, 30 Philistines, and 1,000 men, to mention just a few of his awesome acts. He carried off the gates of Gaza and destroyed the temple of Dagon. He moved into an unparalleled realm of spiritual power and authority—one which the church desires today. But his newfound power did not motivate him to conquer his blatant, sinful, sexual relations with women of other nations. The results of Samson's self-indulgence were deadly.

Every heart, whether regenerate or unregenerate, craves power in one form or another. J. Oswald Sanders says, "Simon coveted the power which he saw Peter exercise and asked, 'Give me also this power. . .' But Peter said to him, 'Your silver perishes with you because you thought you could obtain the gift of God with money.'"[12]

As we move from unfulfillment into fruitfulness, we move into another level of temptation and testing. As God provides the grace of enlargement, influence, and success, we are tempted with ownership attitudes. As God loans us His power, we are tempted to use the power for our own purposes and allow mixture, compromise, and blatant disobedience to go unchecked. We must keep our hunger focused on *the God of power* rather than *the power of God.*

As delays transform into victories, prepare to face your Samson tests. How you respond will leave an eternal imprint on your world, your generation, and the population of His kingdom.

Lessons in Ownership

In this chapter we have discovered that:

• When leaders are fruitful through their own unique giftings, abilities, personalities, methods, and creativity, *ownership* is the result.

• A season of delay in fulfillment is God's

method for exposing and removing our grip, our tightfisted attitude of ownership in order to move us into a new realm of ministry.

• Only when we can die to the vision, do we have the assurance that God owns it. A dead person doesn't have much of a grip!

• God's gifts to us are usually regulated in their extent by our capacity for receiving them.

• Success is a test. What we don't know is what success will do once it has been birthed. What will power do once it has been given life?

• We must focus on God, not the power He can give us.

• God loans us His power, but we are tempted to use the power for our own purposes and allow compromise and blatant disobedience to go unchecked.

• When the power lines get crossed, the Church gets hurt.

Making It Personal

1. Has God given you a vision that you have sweated and toiled for? Will you lay it down to serve another if God asks you to?

2. Have you died to your will and risen to God's? Where do you need to loosen your grip?

3. Are there still areas in your life where your power struggle with the world could cause you to fall into Satan's trap? Ask God to show you.

4. What is your real motive for seeing God's power released in your church, in your ministry, in your life?

Chapter 6

DELAYS DESIGNED
TO STRENGTHEN

$\mathscr{S}$amuel the prophet-judge would lead Israel out of the turbulent times of the judges into the prosperous times of the kings. Samuel would be a king-maker, a king-anointer, and a king-confronter. His mother, Hannah, would be the foundation for his long and influential ministry to Israel. The story of Hannah is another example of delayed promises. Hannah's story is found in 1 Samuel 1:1

through 2:21, and takes place during one of Israel's key historical turning points. Again, God, by His sovereign hand, prepared the way for greatness through a woman's life of pain, sorrow, rejection, and humiliation.

Grace in the Face of Delay

Hannah's experiences offer insights into ministries and churches that are experiencing delays in promised blessings. Hannah was one of two wives of Elkanah. Peninnah, the other wife, had children; Hannah was barren. The name Hannah means grace, graciousness, or favor. And as her name suggests, barrenness had not caused a disgruntled, murmuring, cynical attitude in this woman of character.

Every year Elkanah went up to Shiloh, about a 16-mile journey, to sacrifice and celebrate God's blessing upon their home (1 Sam. 1:3). These festival celebrations were times of rejoicing in God's abundant provisions, blessings, and goodness. But for Hannah, this annual trip was the deepest and darkest hour of her year. It was the time of year Elkanah would praise Peninnah for the sons and daughters she had given him, blessing each child by name. There in the shadows, standing alone, heartbroken, and humiliated, would be Hannah. Elkanah loved Hannah deeply. He would attempt to offer some healing to her by giving her a "double portion" (v. 5) of the sacrifice meat or the harvest offering. But she was barren. No children to bless. No celebration over her offspring.

Peninnah goaded Hannah by pointing out her childlessness, adding to her humiliation. However, the sorrow, humiliation, and attacks only worked in Hannah a deeper grace and graciousness that would be foundational to the awesome ministry of Samuel, the great and wise prophet-judge.

Shame of Unfruitfulness

I'm sure every church and ministry in a season of unfruitfulness can identify with Hannah. Going up to your Shiloh is like attending your particular denomination or movement's annual pastors' conference. It's a time of celebration, rejoicing, testimonies of God's goodness and divine provision. Pastors and church leaders talk openly of church expansion, new building programs, new evangelistic outreaches, new membership ideas. Pastors speak of the pressure of adding multiple services, and you're thinking of your one sparsely attended service. You stand in the shadows hoping the conversation doesn't turn your way: "How's your Sunday attendance? How many new converts have you had this year? What new building programs are you launching?"

Your heart is filled with sorrow and guilt as you question your calling, maybe even your own relationship with God. It is a festival for most, but a funeral for you. Death is creeping into your vision and your faith dwindles as you compare your barren year with the fruitfulness of others.

Attacking While You're Down

Then it happens. The enemy seizes an opportunity, an open window into your soul that is vulnerable to his hellish assault. "Now," he says, "now is the time to shoot my arrows of discouragement, depression, and accusation."

First Samuel 1:6 reads, "And her rival also provoked her severely, to make her miserable, because the Lord had closed her womb." Peninnah is used to attack Hannah in a weak moment. This is a picture of what our enemy, the devil, will do to every Hannah ministry or church.

The Hebrew word for "rival" (*tsarah*) comes from the verb *tsarar* which means to show hostility toward. The noun form is also translated as "adversary or enemy" (Lev. 8:18). We have a rival. It's not other ministries or churches, but the evil kingdom of darkness with all its demonic hosts that are out to destroy our souls. As we see in Luke 4:13, the barren Hannah ministries and churches will encounter this enemy continually, seasonally, at opportune times: "Now when the devil had ended every temptation, he departed from him until an opportune time." The enemy seeks those moments of opportunity, usually when we least expect his arrival. His timing is calculated, strategized, studied, and directed toward these opportune moments (2 Cor. 4:4; Eph. 2:2; 6:10-17; John 12:31; 1 John 5:19).

Opportune times for satanic attack occur:

• When we are experiencing seasons of fruitfulness (Gen. 49:22-26);

• When we take steps to sacrificially serve or give (Gen. 15:11);

- When we have a genuine spiritual break-through (Exod. 14:15-16);

- When we are offering up serious prayer inter-cession (Dan. 9:3-4; 10:12-14);

- When we are leading, but in need of cleansing (Zech. 3:1-6).

Satan's Stomping Ground

Attacks on Hannah came during her visits to the house of the Lord, a unique timing of the enemy. "This went on year after year. When Hannah went up to the house of the Lord, her rival provoked her till she wept and would not eat" (1 Sam. 1:7). Satan provokes us at the time when we should be enjoying God's presence, celebrating God's victories, and ministering to others in the house of the Lord. The attack is on our ground, our place of prayer and worship, our church, our ministry times.

Hannah's rival took special delight in using the

annual pilgrimage to Shiloh as an occasion for continued provocation, badgering Hannah to the point of tears. Just as Elkanah showed his love to Hannah at every sacrificial festival, so did Peninnah repeat her provocation.

Be aware of your enemy's desire to attack when you visit your Shiloh. Shiloh represents several pertinent truths to every leader who is seeking to fulfill God's dream and vision.

Shiloh Is. . .

Shiloh is the center around which activities involving a vision and the appropriating of that vision take place (Josh. 18:1, 8-10; 19:51; 21:2).

Shiloh is the place where God's people gather and give God the praise and glory for keeping every promise He has made to His people. The word, prophecy, encouragement, and discernment are spoken here (Josh. 21:45; 22:9).

Shiloh is the place where Satan is foiled in his attempts to twist the vision for his own purposes, and his strongholds on God's people are broken. There is a special anointing here for discerning God's truth (Josh. 22:10-34).

Shiloh is a place of comfort and peace for God's people (1 Sam. 1:9, 11).

Shiloh is a place to meet God and obtain the unobtainable desires of the heart (1 Sam. 1:17).

Shiloh is a place of sacrifice and returning to God the gift He has placed in our hands (1 Sam. 1:24).

Shiloh is a place where barrenness (spiritual, emotional, and physical) is turned to victory and fruitfulness in God (1 Sam. 2:1-10).

Shiloh is a place where a dedicated prophet of God can grow and mature in the ways of the Lord (1 Sam. 2:11, 18, 21, 26).

Shiloh is a place of vision in a world that cannot

see, a place of plenty in the midst of famine (1 Sam. 3:1-18).

Shiloh is a place where prophets are confirmed as prophets (1 Sam. 3:19, 20).

Shiloh is a place where the Lord appears and is revealed to His prophets by a Living Word (1 Sam. 3:21).

Shiloh is a place from which the word of the Lord goes forth to all the nations (1 Sam. 4:1).[13]

Let your heart be strengthened as you absorb these words: Your God will always pour in more grace, more promises, more healing, and more strength as the enemy seeks to destroy you.

Breaking Delays Through Intercession

If you find yourself identifying with Hannah's sorrow, emotional turmoil, and attack of the enemy, then you must identify with Hannah's turning to the Lord through intercessory prayer. A season of postponement is an opportunity for the devil to attack, but it is also an opportunity to take your brokenness, sorrow, and grief to God with strong, prayerful intercession. First Samuel 1:10 says, "she was in bitterness of soul," but she didn't allow bitter experiences to mark her soul. She journeyed past the bitter taste of barrenness to a place of deep intercessory prayer. Hannah's prayer in her barren state could be a model prayer for every barren ministry or church. The prayer is recorded in 1 Samuel 1:11-19.

The Vow

Then she made a "vow" (v. 11).

Hannah's vow was a reflection of the depth of her desire and her brokenness. This pouring out of prayer by Hannah before God in His house was her vow that she would give up ownership completely and give back this son exclusively for God's use:

O Lord of hosts, if You will indeed look on the affliction of Your maidservant and remember me, and not forget Your maidservant, but will give Your maidservant a male child, then I will give him to the Lord all the days of his life, and no razor shall come upon his head (1 Sam. 1:11).

The Heart Prayer

"Hannah spoke in her heart; only her lips moved" (v. 13).

Hannah's prayer was hidden within the secret compartment of her soul. This would be a prayer birthed out of her distress. Her heart was filled with the words of her rival and hurts of her journey. It would be from this altar she would find the words to pray. These words had been born in sorrow, birthed in her tears and meditated on for years. She prayed "in the presence of God."

Hannah literally entered into and enjoyed the

manifest presence of God during her intercessory prayer times. She had learned that the only place of comfort, encouragement, and renewal was in the presence of Jehovah. This was her hiding place, her place of intimacy, her place of familiar ground. In His presence is where she would find the grace to make a vow, the grace to pour out her heart and never speak out loud. Her prayer was silent because it was deep inside her, mixed with a felt presence of God. She prayed "in her heart" to herself, silently, sacredly, a divine work hidden from the eyes of Eli the high priest.

The Pouring Out of Prayer

"Have poured out my soul before the Lord" (v. 15).

This is a vivid idiom for praying earnestly and passionately before the Lord. Hannah was under a deep "burden" of prayer. She was deeply troubled and "burdened in spirit"; thus she poured out her soul unto God. Hannah's prayer consisted of great sighing, grief, and brokenness all put into words that only her heart could speak. The mouth could not articulate the depth of her petition. She was barren and childless, but she was not prayerless! Her pain found a refuge in prayer, in a specific kind of praying.

It was in this manifest presence of God that Hannah experienced her breakthrough to fruitfulness. Her tragedy would turn to triumph, for prayer had won the victory. No one else could see, but at that moment Hannah was conceiving Samuel in the privacy of her prayer with God. She had learned that prayer is powerful, even when unuttered or unexpressed, sending the secrets of the soul directly to the throne of God.

Petition Granted

"Then Eli answered and said, 'Go in peace, and the

God of Israel grant your petition which you have asked of Him" (v. 17).

Hannah would receive the honor and favor of God requested in her petition. She would no longer be the barren, harassed woman, sorrowful and grieved. She would now be blessed with favor and honor from God. Her intercession would be gloriously fulfilled. From the moment her intercession was finished, her countenance was changed and she was no longer sorrowful, but joyful. She could eat and return to living a happy, fulfilled life:

And [Hannah] said, "Let your maidservant find favor in your sight." So the woman went her way and ate, and her face was no longer sad (v. 18).

The Vow Fulfilled

"As long as he lives he shall be lent to the Lord" (v. 28).

Hannah's season of unfruitfulness was broken and God gave her Samuel, the great prophet-judge of Israel. Hannah fulfilled her vow exactly as she had made it. She took Samuel when he was weaned and presented him to Eli at the Temple (1 Samuel 1:24-28). Hannah then sang her song of thanksgiving, a bursting forth of her grateful heart, a song filled with exaltation to the Lord. The spiritual lyrics of Hannah are equal to any of the Psalms and eloquent with the divine attributes of power, holiness, knowledge, majesty, and grace.

May every unfulfilled ministry and church sing the song of Hannah as a faith declaration to God's intentions for our future.

Hannah's Song: 1 Samuel 2:1-10

My heart rejoices in the Lord; my horn is exalted in the Lord. I smile at my enemies, because I rejoice in Your salvation. No one is holy like the Lord, for there is none besides You, nor is there any rock like our God.

Talk no more so very proudly; let no arrogance come from your mouth, for the Lord is the God of knowledge; and by Him actions are weighed. The bows of the mighty men are broken, and those who stumbled are girded with strength. Those who were full have hired themselves out for bread, and the hungry have ceased to hunger. Even the barren has borne seven, and she who has many children has become feeble. The Lord kills and makes alive; He brings down to the grave and brings up. The Lord makes poor and makes rich; He brings low and lifts up. He raises the poor from the dust and lifts the beggar from the ash heap, to set them among princes and make them inherit the throne of glory. For the pillars of the earth are the Lord's, and He has set the world upon them. He will guard the feet of His saints, but the wicked shall be silent in darkness. For by strength no man shall prevail. The adversaries of the Lord shall be broken in pieces; from heaven He will thunder against them. The Lord will judge the ends of the earth. He will give strength to His king, and exalt the horn of His anointed.

Lessons in Building Strength

In this chapter we have discovered that:

• As in Hannah's case, we can remain free from a disgruntled, murmuring, cynical attitude by leaning on God for strength.

• The temptation to resent others for the delays we experience can be overcome with the knowledge that the powers of hell and darkness are the enemies, not other people, places, or ministries.

• Beware: Your greatest moments of opportunity become the opportune times for Satan's greatest attacks.

- Our rival, the devil, provokes us at the time when we should be enjoying God's presence, celebrating God's victories and ministering to others in the house of the Lord.

- The more the enemy seeks to destroy you, the greater the outpouring of God's grace in your life. God's power to rebuild is always greater than Satan's power to destroy.

- Those encountering delayed fulfillment of promises will find refuge, not in casual inquiries of God, but in deep, heartfelt intercessory prayer.

Making It Personal

1. In what ways is your rival, the kingdom of hell and darkness, attempting to provoke you to bitterness? Is it self-pity? Is it jealousy? Is it unforgiveness?

2. Reflect on the circumstances just prior to

your season of drought or delayed promises. Were you on the crest of an opportunity? If so, what vulnerabilities gave Satan a window through which to attack?

3. How has the enemy sought to steal the joy of your Shiloh? Will you make the choice to enter into a season of praise?

4. What part does intercessory prayer play in your life? Are you a casual inquirer or a promise-keeping, promise-seeking worshiper who is willing to give your heart's desire back to God?

Chapter 7

DELAYS THAT LEAD TO GROWTH

The trip to Fuller Seminary was more than a geographical change for me. As a nondenominational, charismatic pastor, it was an emotional-theological change. I was leaving familiar ground to venture into doctoral-level studies in a seminary. This was highly unusual for the movement of pastors and churches with which I had been affiliated. We believed the local church was the ground for training, and the Bible itself was sufficient for aiding pastors in building great churches. We of course read other books, and our mother church had established a Bible college, but courses on church growth were not offered. We believed God was responsible for growing the church, not human-made ideas compromising the pattern in His Word.

Here I was walking on the campus of Fuller Seminary, seeking to enroll in the doctoral studies in the School of World Missions and the Institute of Church Growth. I was nervous to say the least; doubtful, yet filled with a sense of expectation. I wanted to learn how to grow churches. I didn't want to lack any theological foundations, relevant methodologies, or new innovative ideas. Church growth training here I come!

This was my first encounter with Dr. C. Peter Wagner. I had read his books, but never personally met him, and yet he went out of his way to accompany me in making the rounds to enroll. My first class on church growth was "Your Church and Church Growth," exactly what I desired. The course description read, "This course is designed to make you a more effective Christian leader. As you systematically work through the contents, you will find yourself developing 'church growth eyes.' You will be challenged by new and exciting opportunities for the future."

Church Growth U, Here I Am

I became a serious student of church growth, taking classes and reading more than a hundred books on church growth from every angle and diverse background. I read, wrote papers, talked with church-growth professors and pastors of large, growing churches. The learning process was life changing and ministry changing. I would have the knowledge to change a church from any nongrowth level into a growing church. Church growth philosophy is based on the scriptural assumption that the church is designed to grow, and all other nongrowth ideas are unscriptural excuses.

Those against church growth were very opposed to the dominant thought perceived in church growth: *I can grow my church.* Robert K. Hadnut's *Church Growth Is Not the Point* states the other side. Its protest is directed against all ideas of churchly success as a guarantee of Christian effectiveness. That means the point of the church's existence is whether the church is true to the gospel, not whether it grows numerically. Hadnut has the following to say:

One final slogan that contains a lot of unexamined and questionable assumptions is church growth. Its philosophy undergirds a great deal of thinking and planning to do with the church's mission in the world. Perhaps your church is committing itself to an outreach program and you see this as a heavenly mandate to increase and multiply. But let's be clear that witness and numerical growth are not the same. As I read the New Testament, the Lord's commission to His church is to be faithful in witness, not necessarily successful in growing. You could say that whenever growing is spoken of in the New Testament church, the implied subject of the sentence is God, as in 1 Corinthians 3:7. It is God's church we are talking about and He alone can produce the growth.[14]

In the arguments for and against church growth, both sides have biblical insights. The proper combination for healthy church growth is the power of God and the responsibility of man. The key, of course, is to use both, with balance and wisdom, to bring about desired growth. The frustration is when a pastor who has a nongrowing church, a barren church, puts into practice all the points from church-growth literature and does not see results. This is when knowledge of principles and patterns falls hurtfully short and the mystery of church growth is encountered. "I have done everything I was supposed to do. I followed the plan carefully and there are no apparent results." This dilemma is what I have come to describe as "The Elizabeth Factor."

When You're Doing Everything You Know

Zacharias and Elizabeth were doing all the rights things in the right way with a righteous motive. They were model examples of following the pattern God had laid down, yet they were without child:

And they were both righteous before God, walking in all the commandments and ordinances of the Lord blameless. But they had no child, because Elizabeth was barren, and they were both well advanced in years (Luke 1:6, 7).

Elizabeth's childlessness was not caused by a

lack of righteousness or obedience before or unto God. "Righteous before God" means that when they were standing before God's judgment bar, they received His sentence of approval. But to be childless brought sorrow and often shame, representing the result of God's withholding His blessing and favor, or the consequence of hidden sin or rebellion.

Zacharias and Elizabeth were in leadership positions, priests of the Tabernacle, serving according to their order. They were also genuinely godly, humble, and righteous in all ways. They were the perfect couple for God to shower His blessings upon, but Scripture says, "They were without child."

Moving from the Knowledge Part to the God Part

The name Zacharias means "the Lord remembers"; Elizabeth's name means "my God is an absolutely faithful one," or "my God is an oath." Zacharias and Elizabeth had decided to trust God as the faithful God who remembers all His promises to us and for us. They were not moved by their childlessness and had no knowledge of why barrenness prevailed in their marriage.

The Elizabeth Factor describes those ministries or churches that have done everything they know to be fruitful, successful, and influential in a righteous manner, yet without apparent results. Understanding church-growth principles, evangelism ideas, and how to have a successful church are only part of the true picture. There is also the God-part, the hidden part, the sovereign will of God being worked out quietly and secretly. The timetable is in God's hands; the purpose of God is to be fulfilled in the fullness of time.

A church may be without numerical growth and still be blessed and used of God while having no hidden sins to deal with. A church may also be unfruitful because of its poor leadership, violations of basic

New Testament principles, hidden wickedness, or failure to handle the generation slippage. Delays in growth may be God-sent and God-allowed, or may be caused by obvious spiritual flaws. The Elizabeth Factor, however, is when churches are doing most things well (good leadership, fervent prayer, righteous behavior, honoring God in humility, relevant cultural methodology) and yet are not seeing the desired growth: "There are no new converts or very few converts in our church. Year after year we can't break the 100-people barrier (or the 500-people barrier or the 1,000-people barrier). I'm doing everything I know to do, and there is still an invisible wall!"

The Elizabeth Factor shows what is behind the scenes in God's timing for certain breakthroughs and what we can do if we face a similar set of circumstances.

When Time Appears to Be Working Against You

The timing factor of God's dealings, provisions,

and answers to prayer is absolutely unpredictable and unexplainable. Have you given your best years to a ministry or a church only to realize that your time has run out? It's gone, history, never to be repeated. It's over. All those years of serving, preaching, sacrificing, proving, and believing, and now the years have come and gone without the vision being fulfilled.

Are you close to the age of retirement? Are you moving from your 40s to your 50s, realizing that the many things you have dreamed about are almost—if not for sure—impossible now? Are you well advanced in years in comparison to what you desire to see and what you actually have? Did you set high and lofty goals according to the age chart and find yourself falling behind, so far behind now that it is an impossibility to fulfill those goals?

I never wanted to accept the status quo. I always desired God's best, the highest goal, the achiever's mind-set. J. B. Phillips paraphrases Philippians 1:10: "I want you to be able always to recognize the highest and the best." I have tried to press toward the mark of the high calling, setting high goals with excellence as a hallmark. But now, time has run out. It would take a miracle for me to accomplish what I thought to be a God-vision.

This is the Elizabeth Factor: "well advanced in years" (Luke 1:7). You feel time is working against you every day. Take heart. Remember: Benjamin Franklin was 81 years old when he helped to create the Constitution of the United States; George Bernard Shaw was 94 when one of his plays was first performed; Golda Meir was 71 when she was elected Prime Minister of Israel!

Divine Answers During Routine Ministry

The class to which Zacharias belonged was having its regular week of priestly service in the sanctuary (Luke 1:8). This priestly service was completed by Zacharias with faithfulness, respect to God, and respect to his calling as a priest. According to the custom of the priesthood, his "lot" fell to burn incense. It was the custom to cast lots for this highest daily task of burning the incense on the golden altar in the holy place. Only once in a priest's life could he be granted this high privilege.

The priest would sprinkle frankincense upon the coals, causing a cloud to arise, spreading fragrance. His task was the symbolic representation of the rising up to God of the prayers and longings of the people. The priest would then, while the incense cloud was present, offer up prayers consisting of thanksgiving for blessings received and supplication for the peace of Israel. The people who gathered outside the Temple would at the same time prostrate themselves and offer prayers.

The divine interruption happened while Zacharias performed his sacred duties as he had been performing them for more than 30 years. For more than 30 years nothing supernatural had happened, and there was nothing extraordinary about his ministry or his name. This day would be different:

"And there appeared unto him an angel of the Lord standing on the right side of the altar of incense. And when Zacharias saw him, he was troubled, and fear fell upon him. But the angel said unto him, Fear not, Zacharias: for thy prayer is heard; and thy wife Elizabeth shall bear thee a son, and thou shalt call his name John. And thou shalt have joy and gladness; and many shall rejoice at his birth. For he shall be great in the sight of the Lord. . . ." (Luke 1:11-15).

Prayers are often heard by God long before He sends the answer. This was God's timing—the time He selected to grant all those fervent petitions of years past. God's timing brought a divine purpose, provision, and promise far greater than Elizabeth and Zacharias could ever have imagined.

It is important to grasp that when unfruitfulness, delays, and time are against you, you must keep doing the things God has already given you to do. Keep preaching, keep praying, keep serving, keep sacrificing, keep overseeing. For in the routine, the mundane, the normal, the common, the everyday, will come a supernatural intervention. The key is commitment in the normal, commitment in the common, commitment to burn incense for the people whether your prayers are answered or not.

Press on, fellow Christian. Your season of unfruitfulness will break, and when it does, your destiny will collide with His timing to produce more than you expected for a purpose that will far exceed your hopes.

Lessons in Growth

In this chapter we have discovered that:

• The proper combination for healthy church growth is the power of God and the responsibility of man.

• Trusting His sovereignty is realizing that our timetable is in God's hands.

• Many who have gone before us have experienced their greatest achievements in the last lap of their lives.

• When unfruitfulness and time are against you, you must keep doing the things God has already given you to do. God interrupts those who are faithful in the routine and mundane with supernatural interventions.

• "Impossible" is just a word. God will not be constrained by man's word; rather, He fulfills His own Word in His time for His kingdom purposes.

• When God breaks the season of drought and delays, our destinies far exceed our past petitions.

Making It Personal

1. Can you identify with Zacharias and Elizabeth? Do your goals and dreams seem to have surpassed their season of fruition? Will you keep looking to God?

2. Do you feel as though life has passed you by? If so, has the story of Zacharias and Elizabeth convinced you that God can still burst forth into your ordinary circumstances with a baton of victory you never expected to carry?

3. In what ways have you developed attitudes that are resistant to serving in the mundane, routine, and even boring tasks of ministry?

4. Do others see in you a "Zacharias/Elizabeth" model of faithfulness? If not, will you choose to change?

NOTES

1. Joseph Stowell, *Shepherding the Church into the Twenty-First Century* (Colorado Springs: Victor Books, 1994), p. 12.

2. H. C. Leupold, *Exposition of Genesis* (Grand Rapids: Baker Books, 1944), Vol. II, p. 701.

3. Norman Grubb, Rees Howells, *Intercessor* (Fort Washington, Pa.: Christian Literature Crusade, 1993), p. 71.

4. Ralph Turnbull, *A Minister's Obstacles* (Grand Rapids: Baker Publishing, 1972—originally published by Fleming H. Revel, 1946), p. 13.

5. Joseph Stowell, *Shepherding the Church into the Twenty-First Century* (Colorado Springs: Victor Books, 1994), p. 151.

6. *Webster's New Twentieth Century Dictionary—2nd Edition*, (U.S.A.: Collins World Publishers, 1978).

7. Jack Hayford, *Pastors of Promise* (Ventura, Calif.: Regal, 1997), p. 161.

8. Ralph G. Turnbull, *A Minister's Obstacles* (Grand Rapids: Baker Books, 1972—originally published by Fleming H. Revel, 1946), p. 37.

9. Ibid., p. 34.

10. H. C. Leupold, *Exposition of Genesis—Vol. II* (Grand Rapids: Baker Books, 1987), p. 815.

11. Charles Stanley, *The Blessings of Brokenness* (Grand Rapids: Zondervan), p. 13.

12. J. Oswald Sanders, *Spiritual Lessons* (Chicago: Moody Press), p. 55.

13. Carl Townsend, *Strategic Visions for the Evangelization of Portland* (Portland, Ore., March 31, 1995).

14. Robert K. Hadnut, *Church Growth Is Not the Point* (N.Y.: HarperCollins, 1975), p. 33.